Mary Magdalene Speaks from Heaven Book 2:

A Divine Revelation

Nicola Whitehall

Matthew Robert Payne

Please visit http://personal-prophecy-today.com to sow into Matthew's writing ministry, to request a personal prophecy or life coaching, or to contact him.

Cover design by akira007 at fiverr.com.

Book design by WildBlu Design at darla@wildbludesign.com.

Editing by Lisa Thompson at www.writebylisa.com

You can email Lisa at writebylisa@gmail.com for your editing needs.

Published by Christian Book Publishing USA. The opinions expressed by the author are not necessarily those of Christian Book Publishing USA. Christian Book Publishing USA is committed to excellence in the publishing industry. Copyright ©2018 by Christian Book Publishing USA. All rights reserved.

Paperback ISBN: 978-1-925845-01-3

First Edition: July 2018

0 1 2 3 4 5 6 7 8 9 10

Dedication by Nicola

I want to dedicate my part of this book to my dear friend, Matthew Robert Payne. I have known him for almost a year now, and my close friendship with him brings a great deal of richness and a lot of laughter and fun to my life. He gives to others and makes time for them, putting other people first even when he is suffering and struggling himself. He is an inspiration to me in how he has persevered, and in the midst of his trials, he has always been willing to serve the Lord.

He has truly put his talents to work even through what has come against him. I appreciate his loving, kind, tender, and generous heart of humility despite his great revelations and relationship with God. He makes time for me, even when he is busy, with a caring and listening ear. He communicates naturally in his easy-going manner and encourages me. He always sees the good in me when I don't see it in myself. I appreciate how he has shared his life with me and allowed me to speak into his life.

His knowledge and understanding have opened up a new realm for me in hearing from and talking to saints and angels in a way I never thought possible. His solid, practical, and life-giving biblical teaching has caused me to change and grow in many aspects of my Christian life.

Thank you, Matthew, for everything you are and all you have done for me. I love you, and you are one of my best friends, and you are so valuable and important to me. I wish you every success in the future. May God prosper you in everything you do and lead you forward into the great destiny he has for you. It will soon be time for Jesus to shine through you to the world in a much greater measure!

Dedication by Matthew

I want to dedicate this book to my friend Wendy. She has been a dear friend to me and has set me free in some areas. She is a great support to me. She continues to set people free every day of her life. I am enriched by knowing her.

Introduction by Nicola

When Matthew first asked me to coauthor this book with him, I wasn't sure if it was the right thing to do. I had been working on my memoir for almost two years and had come to a standstill. I struggled with wanting to finish my original book before tackling a new project.

I was besieged by five-hour anxiety attacks when writing about personal and emotional subjects in my memoir. Matthew then suggested that this could be a worthwhile project, as it would be easier to write about something less personal and emotional. He observed that in this way, I could have a book under my belt.

When I decided that the opportunity was too great to miss out on, I had no idea how to go about interviewing a saint from heaven. I knew Matthew had a portal in his house where supernatural visitors passed back and forth, but did I? I prepared nine questions for myself and some questions for Matthew. I decided that if Matthew had come up with the idea, God was probably behind it. I left the logistics of it in God's hands and waited to see what would happen.

A few days before the interview commenced, I saw a vision with my spiritual eyes: Jesus with his arm around Mary Magdalene in the right corner of my bedroom. She was short, petite, and perhaps a size 8 or a 10 with very long brown hair trailing down her back. A short time later, Jesus and Mary appeared directly in front of my bed facing each other. Jesus placed a ring on Mary's finger. It was if Jesus were introducing me to Mary and conveying to me the immense respect, love, and care that he had for his beloved saint.

Not long after, I had a night of insomnia. I watched a live one-hour webinar from Florida, and I participated in taking communion. It was 4:30 a.m., and I heard God say in my spirit that he wanted to speak to me. I took out my journal to record his words. He said a few things and then said, "Would you like to talk to Mary Magdalene now?"

I replied, "Do you mean just to chat or to ask my questions to her?"

"You could try asking the questions and see how it goes," God answered.

It was about 5:00 a.m., and I took out my voice recorder. I had discussed with Matthew that I would record an interview with a saint in the same manner as he did. This was because God had spoken through me once, and I knew hearing and having a supernatural voice speaking through me took some concentration.

I sensed Mary by my bed with my spiritual eyes, so I began asking my questions. At some point, she must have hopped into me because I began speaking in Mary's distinct voice and personality. After fifty minutes was up, I felt like celebrating. I had done it.

I couldn't wait to tell Matthew what had happened that night. Of course, he was thrilled and wanted to know my questions for Mary and some of the answers. But I waited until I had transcribed the interview and completed two rounds of edits before I showed him. He loved what Mary said and interviewed Mary with his questions later that night. I was amazed at her answers when he played his interview with Mary to me.

I met Mary a few times in 2017. She appeared when I was in distress and put her arms around me and comforted me, but I didn't know her well. After this interview, she appeared once while I was at the movies with a friend, watching *God's Not Dead.* She showed up with Jesus when I was walking to a group I was nervous about attending. She and Jesus stayed with me throughout the group session. She is such a delight to know as a saint, and I love her very much.

The only other saint that I have talked with extensively is John who called himself John the Revelator. He talked with me in the early hours of the morning of August 16, 2017, and I recorded about three pages of what he said to me.

I was amazed at how Matthew spoke so clearly to saints and interviewed them, and you might be too. But I write the above so that you know that having this experience isn't beyond the reach of any of us. I am a normal person with normal experiences, and I had never had saints communicate with me until I read Matthew's books. Through reading Matthew's books, I learned that saints and angels speak through you just like the Holy Spirit does. Anyone can have this experience. If you can hear from God, you can hear from saints. And if you can't hear from God, you can easily learn. Just buy a book on the subject, such as Matthew's *How to Hear God's Voice: Keys to Conversational Two-Way Prayer.*

Or you could investigate Communion with God Ministries, Four Keys to Hearing God's Voice. You can find the free resources at *www.cwgministries.org* on the group's home page.

I hope you enjoy this interview with Mary as much as I enjoyed recording it. It is only my first interview with a saint, so I was overwhelmed much of the time. Her answers might seem short, as I was eager to finish the questions. This was a new experience; I was a novice. Mary has some priceless words she wants to share with you, the reader, and I hope you are blessed and touched by them.

TABLE OF CONTENTS

TABLE OF CONTENTS continued

Nicola's Questions

1 *How do you feel about being here today?*

I'm very honored to be here today to speak to you and to love on you when you're going through a hard time. I'm here to be your friend and to help you however you need me to help you. I'm looking forward to answering your questions. I'm very excited about this interview. You're the first person besides Matthew who has interviewed me, and I'm really excited to be speaking through your voice and through your heart. I really appreciate and like who you are and who you are going to be in the Lord as the Lord develops you further.

Nicola: Thank you for that answer, Mary Magdalene.

2 *Can you tell me what Jesus is like?*

Jesus is a very funny character. He really makes me laugh. He's been so close to me on this earth. He truly loves me, and he died for me on the cross. I saw him die, which made me very sad, and I cried for days afterward. But it was a privilege to be able to support him while he was there dying on the cross. I knew he needed me, and though it was hard for me, I had to be there. I wanted to be there for him because he was my close friend. And if he had allowed me to be, I would have been more than that, but that wasn't meant to be. He was meant to die for the sins of the world so that everyone could be his bride. I appreciated the opportunity to be by his side and to follow him and learn and grow from knowing him.

I was a companion to him and a friendly face for him to look at. When he was feeling low, I would sometimes giggle, laugh, and have fun with him, and he would cheer up. He wanted to die on the cross for the sins of mankind, but he was sad, and he shared that with me. I was sad too, but I put on a brave face, and I stayed positive for him. I kept reminding him of his purpose and what a wonderful person he was, and I just kept things light with him. I laughed with him, and I prodded and poked at him in fun. I told jokes, and he really appreciated that. He enjoyed my lighthearted banter and the sisterly love I had for him. That really helped him when he went to the cross. He was distracted then, which was understandable, as anyone would be very nervous and have a lot of anticipation or maybe even dread about going to the cross. But I could support Jesus and lighten his load by being a sister to him. I helped him by being loving and kind and keeping the mood light when it could have been very serious, dour, and difficult for him.

Is there anything more you want to say about what Jesus is like?

He's such a cool dude. He's really friendly and loving. He loves everybody. He doesn't look at some people and hate them or despise them. He doesn't love some people more than others. He distributes his love evenly. He has friends who are closer to him and people he shares intimate secrets with. But he loves everyone equally. He loves every heart. He loved the hardest Pharisees, and he even loved those who hated him, those who whipped him, and those who caused him the most pain. He talked to me and told me he was able to love those people even as they were causing him great pain and were torturing him. He was so loving and was always thinking of others.

He was always putting others first and thinking about how he could minister to people and how he could bless and teach them. He thought about how he could make everything we did into a teaching lesson. He had a lot of fun as well, but he was able to turn everything that happened into something we could learn from. This was true even if it seemed negative: lost money or if we had no money or whatever problem came up. He was able to perform a miracle and solve the problem.

3

What are some of the main lessons you learned on earth?

I learned to be close to Jesus, and when he left, I learned to be close to the Holy Spirit. I learned that if I was close to Jesus, I could achieve anything. I could go through anything; I could endure anything. When he was there or when the Holy Spirit was with me, I could get through whatever trial I faced with help from heaven. I learned to rely on and lean into the Holy Spirit or into Jesus. I learned to commit myself to him. I learned to be sold out completely to him and not to worry about what others thought about me. That was one of my main lessons.

I used to worry about how the crowds saw me, even when I was sneaking up and listening to Jesus's sermons. I was very worried about how people perceived me and how they'd judge me. I was focused on other people's views of me and worried about their negative opinions. I was worried that Jesus would have a bad reputation because I followed him. I was worried about the rich people I served and what they thought of me following Jesus. But I learned not to worry about what people thought. I learned to trust in who Jesus said I was. I learned to trust in his love for me. I learned to know that when I could experience his all-consuming love for me, it banished any fear of others' opinions, any fear of what they thought of me, or any worry that they thought badly of me. That was because I had this one man, this one man who loved me and died for me.

He literally died for me. He died for the world, but when I personalize it for myself, he loved me so deeply, and he was so sold out to me as a person. He gave me everything that he had. He taught me everything that he knew; he loved me with everything he had, and I knew it.

I came to know that the Father loved me with everything he had, and I knew that the Holy Spirit would help me. The Holy Spirit loved me with everything he had, and so I knew I didn't need to fear other people's opinions. I didn't need to worry about what others thought, because I was so secure and so rooted in what he thought of me and so overwhelmed by what he did for me, the love he had for me. I was there. I was amazed that he would go through what I saw him go through. I saw some of the whipping. I saw them tear through his back. I saw the agony on his face, and it nearly killed me, but I knew that he was going to go through that for me because I had talked to him about it.

After that, I was undone. There was nothing that I would not do for him. I wanted to give my world to him. I wanted to give him everything I had: all my love, all my service, and all my blessings. I wanted to serve him by serving and loving other people. Before he left, I wanted to serve him, but after he left, I wanted to love the people that he loved and serve others. If he could love like that, then so could I.

He gave me an example, something that I could hold onto. He gave me a model of what love was and how someone could love another person and how someone could love and forgive another person like me who had committed so many great sins. He gave me such a great example that I could follow, and I was just so blessed to see that example. One of the greatest things I learned from Jesus was how to love. His love washed away my fear of what others thought, and I became totally devoted and sold out to him.

>Nicola: Wow, Mary; that was great. Thank you. I love the answers you are giving.

4 *Which of the twelve disciples did you get along best with, and what did you talk about on earth, and what do you talk about in heaven now?*

Well, I'm sure that it comes as no surprise to you, Nicola, but I was closest to John. He was with me when we stood before Jesus at the cross. He was one of Jesus's closest disciples, the one that Jesus loved, according to John 13:23. He practiced the presence of love with Jesus. We discussed Jesus and talked about how he would suffer. Besides me, he understood what would happen to Jesus. We used to talk about how we could support Jesus more and how we could reach more people and how we could be like him: imitate him and represent him well. Sometimes we talked about whom we should help and how the money should be spent that came into the ministry.

I was closest to John, and we talked a lot about Jesus and his great love. If you don't know Jesus, you don't know how loving he is, but John and I both had his example to watch. We had both experienced Jesus's love for us, which was what we discussed. We discussed his love and his devotion to his Father. I especially saw him spend a lot of time with his Father. Sometimes John was asleep, but I always saw Jesus get up early and spend time with the Father. John and I discussed his devotion to the Father and how we could be devoted to the Father as well. But we often just watched Jesus and listened to him, and we saw how he lived. After he left, we followed his example.

Yes, in heaven we talk about the following: what will happen on earth, our favorite people, our favorite things on earth, and memories of old times. You know, you might think that nearly two thousand years later, we would have stopped talking about what happened on earth. But we sometimes still reminisce, laugh together, and joke. We talk about the fun times we had, the times of joy, and the times of laughter. We have to remember those things because the life of Jesus was filled with much sorrow. We had a chance to grow close to him. He dealt with a lot of hurt that he had to work through, and I listened to him when he talked about it.

In heaven, we have a real knowing. We—John and I—know each other so well. We talk about some of the miracles we did, about what we did together, and about some of the people we loved on the earth at that time. We also talk about some of the people on earth now whom we love, those whom we will minister to and whom we will mentor. We discuss people we are appearing to at the moment on earth. John and I sometimes come and talk to people together because he and I were the closest to Jesus in love. We sometimes minister as a duo because I'm the feminine, and he's the masculine, and we hold different strengths. We have different perspectives. When we mentor someone on earth, sometimes the person needs to be talked to by a man, and sometimes he or she needs to be talked to by a woman. We take turns and talk to the person.

In many ways, we operate like the angels do, except we've had experience as humans on the earth, which makes us uniquely able to understand the person we are ministering to and communicating with. We talk to some people who are being tortured in prisons or who are in some of the persecuted countries and are locked away and some whom nobody else even knows about. We are talking to them; we're showing them how to love in that situation. We're showing them how to have grace.

I recently appeared before someone in prison who was being tortured, and through the power of the Holy Spirit, I showed the person what I saw when Jesus was whipped with the cat-o'-nine-tails. I showed the person what he went through. This strengthened the person and helped the person go through what the person had to suffer for Christ. I was there, and I put my arms around the person and loved the person.

Sometimes when they need advice, John appears. He gives them manly advice and sometimes says some of the harder things they need to hear, such as messages of "pull yourself up by your bootstraps." An example of what he says might be, "You are going through a hard situation, but you have to endure. It's part of your walk in Christ, part of what you need to go through. Your reward in heaven is great. You can endure this. Look at what Jesus endured. You can endure this. One day, you'll be free, and you'll share Jesus's gospel around the earth."

We are already mentoring some people on earth, and John and I work together as a team. We show people, particularly Christians who are suffering greatly, how to love and how to forgive those who are harming or persecuting them.

Nicola: Wow, Mary. That was an amazing answer to my question.

5 How do you feel about serving God and Jesus in heaven?

I absolutely love serving God the Father and Jesus in heaven. I love them so much, and it's such a joy and a privilege to serve the ones who created, formed, and loved me and who love me still. It's so amazing, when your life was previously full of sin, to have your sins washed away. It makes you want to love with all your heart until every inch of you is squeezed out like an orange on a juicer. Every inch of liquid is squeezed out to be used for the Father's good purpose.

I love serving the Father as an ambassador where I appear at ceremonies and similar events. It's such an honor to serve the Father and Jesus in heaven. As you know, I am a dancer in heaven, and I know you like dancing, Nicola. I have perfected my dancing skills although I can always learn more. I'm learning choreography, how to dance to choreography, and how to structure dances. I'm also designing some dances that will be performed in the throne room.

There will be some large-scale dances that will be part of a huge dance opera. It is similar to what dance choreographers, such as Michael Parmenter, do in your country. Many dancers will be on stage—well, not a stage but in the throne room. They will do an amazing dance, almost like the equivalent of a mass in music. It will be huge, like a grand musical. I am doing the choreography along with some of my dancer friends, including Matthew's sister, Karen. We are organizing and structuring the groups. We're dancing and choreographing the dance, and I'm leading the dancers.

Karen has a very prominent position in helping choreograph the dancers in their formations and in everything that will happen in heaven. It's our way of honoring God. We love to express ourselves emotionally and physically through dance and use our whole bodies to worship the King. It's so uplifting to be able to honor him like that. The whole host of heaven will come and join us and sing in the choir. We will sing and dance with an orchestra and an organ. Your friend Jack will play the organ, a grand organ. There will be a full orchestra with some pop and electronic music like you would have on earth along with some electric guitars, keyboards, and synthesizers.

There are all sorts of instruments. It will be a massive dance opera, such as what Mark Morris would do in America. These types of shows happen in heaven as well. We have these great performances, and it's such an honor to dance for our King and Lord. We are doing our very best to give a stellar and amazing performance. The Holy Spirit inspires and guides us in what steps to do and what music to use. We have composers who are composing music, and the angels and people are singing in the choirs and playing instruments.

We so enjoy doing this at the moment, and the people in heaven love being a part of it. I wanted to mention something we're working on at the moment. This will be replicated; there will be many more operas and grand dance operas in heaven. They will be done in the throne room because the Lord needs to be glorified on a grand scale. We really want to use our talents for him because he has given us those talents.

We have developed and honed our skills, and we have worked on the steps and spent hours choreographing and creating structures, formations, and systems. The dancers and musicians are rehearsing separately. Later, we get together and rehearse as a group. We want to glorify the Lord and bless the whole of heaven, all the people who will come and watch this opera. I'm not going to tell you what it will be about, because it will be a surprise. You'll see it in heaven one day. You'll see a video of it, or you might see a different large-scale opera that I have helped produce with Karen, your friend Jack, and some other people, including Michael Jackson. Those are some of the people you know who are a part of this.

I wanted to give you an example of what we're doing in heaven at the moment to glorify our Lord and King. Jesus is helping us, and his Holy Spirit is giving us creative ideas. We're flowing in the Spirit and working hard to do something really great that will glorify him.

Nicola: Mary, thank you so much for your lovely answer about the musical operas and dance operas you're working on in heaven. It sounds exciting. I never thought they would do things like that in heaven, but of course, if they do them on earth, they would do them in heaven.

Okay, Mary, the next question will be my hardest one, but I'm just going to trust God. I'm going to pray that the Holy Spirit would help me relax for this question where I'll really need to allow you to speak through me. I'm a little nervous, so I would like to ask the Holy Spirit and Delilah, my guardian angel, to calm my nerves and for the Holy Spirit to fill me with his presence so that I can hear clearly what you have to say and not be stressed or worried about it.

11

I must have read in one of Matthew's books that Jesus told a lot of stories to illustrate his sermons. There must be a favorite story you have or a story that you can remember. I know he told you stories in heaven as well, but could you tell me a story that he told on earth that wasn't in the Bible?

6 What was one of the stories Jesus told on earth?

Yes, Nicola, you do not need to be worried about this question. I'm more than happy to tell you about a story Jesus told on earth. He told us a story about a poor widow. She was very sad because she had lost her husband, and she had no way to provide for herself and her family. A fisherman came along, and he gave her a fish and said, "If you open this fish's mouth, a coin will be inside, which will be enough money for you to live on for a month." She opened the fish's mouth, and the fish had a coin inside its mouth that was enough for her to live on for a month.

This widow didn't have much. She had several children she had to look after, and she didn't know what she was going to do. She prayed to the Lord and asked him for help. She still didn't know what she was going to do. When a month had passed, she'd spent the coin and paid all her expenses. The fisherman came to her door again and asked, "What do you need?"

She responded, "I need more money and provision. I have children; I need a husband and help. I don't have any family; I don't have anywhere to go. I don't have anything to do for work, and I have babies I have to rear and take care of. I don't have anywhere I can go and work and bring the babies."

The fisherman said, "Come out with me while I fish." So she went out with him on the boat.

One of the fishermen in the boat knew someone who was rich with a large house. He said, "Come and visit my friend." The fisherman took her to meet his friend, and this man with the large house took her in and put her up for a month. During that time, he paid all her expenses, and her children were well-fed and properly clothed. She didn't have to worry about anything. She just needed to relax, and she tried to enjoy her life.

The wealthy man was older, and he had a son. The son came in and asked, "Do you want to marry again?" She said that she did, and a relationship developed between them. He became her husband, and they moved out of the house together. This younger man who had taken the woman in had some of the wealth of his father. The young man provided for her and her eleven children. She had many children, and she had a new husband and a new house.

Her husband went out and worked. In today's world, we'd consider him a businessman. Jesus said, "If this woman can live by faith, if she can have nothing and yet obey the people God sent to her, and if she can trust, how much more can you trust me when I lead, guide, and direct you? This poor woman lost her husband. She had no money to live on. She could not work because she had eleven young children. She was probably going to lose her rental house because she couldn't afford it. She wasn't able to provide for herself.

So how much more can you trust me to direct you and to provide for you? I provided for that widow; I sent that fisherman; I guided her to the boat with the fisherman who knew the other wealthy man. I sent the wealthy man's son into that house to marry her and give her a house and money to support her children. I provided her with everything she needed. I gave her the desire of her heart because she didn't give up. She followed the instructions that the people I sent to her gave her. I send the Holy Spirit to you, and all you need to do is follow his instructions and do what he says, and I will provide for you. All you need to do is be obedient. This was really a story about obedience."

She knew the Holy Spirit was guiding this fisherman on the boat. It made no sense for a woman with eleven children, including babies, to go on a fishing boat. When one of the other fishermen saw her plight, the Holy Spirit moved on him and gave him the idea to talk to her about the wealthy man with extra rooms in his house who could take her in. Then the Holy Spirit moved on the wealthy man's son, who was looking for a wife. He fell in love with her and wanted to provide for her and give her a house and an income. Jesus was saying that this is an example of how the Lord works, of how he can use unusual means to provide for you. All you have to do is be obedient to what he asks you to do. When you're trusting in him, he will provide everything you need.

Nicola: Wow, Mary. That was amazing. I took a step of faith because I didn't know how I was going to come up with an answer. You came up with it, but it was scary for me because I didn't have a clue as to what you were going to say.

7 *Whom do you have the most compassion, love, and concern for on earth?*

I want to talk to you about those I love on earth. I love the people, my family. The family I had before I met Jesus were people working in the service industry, people who worked as prostitutes. People don't understand just how broken, needy, and desperate those individuals were. The sex workers needed money, and not all of the people I was friends with were high-class prostitutes or could earn a high income like I did. I made a lot of money, and I could help finance the early church. I used to help supplement the income of my friends who struggled. This was even before I knew Jesus because I knew their troubles; I knew their pain, and I knew how they felt about their bodies being used over and over and over again.

When you go through that situation, even though you earn a lot of money, something in you dies. You tell yourself that you're living the good life, that you can do anything you want, go anywhere you please, take time off, and do what you want to do. But your soul is dead, and a part of you hates what you're doing. There's no peace. There are highs and lows. You experience highs when you have large amounts of money and a sense of power over the men who are yearning to be with you and spend time with you. At those times, you love the power and the influence you have.

You tell yourself that this is fantastic and this is what you want, but you feel so broken, so empty, and dead inside. It's hard to be honest with yourself. For a long time, I wasn't honest with myself, and Jesus changed me and helped me to see my real state and condition before I turned to him. He helped expose what my life really was. It wasn't the life I wanted or the life God wanted for me. He had so much more for me. I just love my sisters and my brothers on earth who don't yet know the Lord but who are stuck in that same lifestyle. They don't know that God has so much more for them. He has so many great plans for them, and I know that he wants to scoop them up and hold them in his arms and remove them from the situation they're in.

This includes trafficked boys, girls, and babies and those who are so-called willingly working in the prostitution industry. Yes, I am concerned for those who are sex slaves, those who are working in the prostitution industry, because really all my brothers and sisters in that industry are slaves. They're slaves to their sin, to the master enemy, to the one who wants to capture their souls and plunge them into darkness for the rest of their lives and for eternity. They are captives, and they don't know it. They don't know there's so much more for them: healing and love so great they can hardly even comprehend it. If someone could just tell them about that love, if they just knew that love, then they would find a way out of what they are doing.

They could trust the Holy Spirit like that widow in the story I just told you. If they could trust the Holy Spirit for provision, if they left prostitution, they would find a God who loves them, a God who would provide for them. They could follow the direction of the Holy Spirit and allow God to heal their souls and allow him to resurrect them from the death within them, the darkness in them. Jesus loves them so much, and so do I.

So who do I care about the most? I care most about my sisters and brothers in the sex trade. I don't think anybody in that industry has a choice. Whatever reason has led them into that place or state, they don't really know any better. Those are the people who are on my heart, the people I identify with. My heart goes out to all of these people: the people who are there by choice or some of the children, the dear children, who are taken at a young age or satanically ritually abused.

You know I have a heart for Matthew; I have such a heart for him. You know I spend time with him. I understand him, and I understand the brokenness in his life. I'm a great mentor to him and a great supporter, encourager, and comforter to him because he identifies with me and with where I've come from. He is going to be used mightily to help those in the sex trade. He doesn't know this yet, but he's going to have a hand in what happens in the future to those people who are trapped in this industry. Both he and you have a part to play, Nicola. God wants to use many people around the world today who have some idea of what it's like to be abused. God wants these people to help others who are trapped and tormented by the enemy's power. Many have tormented souls, and they don't know they're tormented, because they're so used to living that way, and they don't know any different. Those are the people I have the most compassion for, Nicola.

Nicola: Thank you, Mary; that was an amazing answer.

17

8 *What are your role and the role of others in heaven to prepare for the great harvest of souls that is coming on earth?*

Well, Nicola, a lot of things will happen on this earth, and I can't tell you them all now. A lot of them will take the enemy by surprise, so he doesn't have a clue what's coming. He knows something's coming, but he doesn't know what. It is similar to how it is with the rest of the world. Suffice it to say that we are preparing in heaven. We are making ready for the Marriage Supper of the Lamb. The angels are being trained.

Our role in preparing for the coming harvest is to invite people to heaven, invite people to experience heaven on earth. We are trying to bring heaven to earth as you have heard Kat Kerr say. We're trying to awaken the people of the earth. We're connected with the people on earth more than ever, and as time advances, this connection will continue to increase. We will interact with them more and more in increased communication as their awareness rises. We are spending more time trying to connect with people. We are not only glorifying the Father in heaven; we are not only standing at the portals and praying for people on earth. We're actively trying to get their attention. The Holy Spirit operates and tries to awaken people to what will happen on earth. He tries to awaken them from their sleep. He's trying to get people out of their ruts and where they are stuck. He's trying to get people to move and witness for the Lord.

The Lord, the Holy Spirit, is sending us down to different people, and we are trying to awaken them. We are trying to direct them and show people the paths the Lord has for them. As we direct and align people with the book of life and with God's purposes for them, they can more fully come into alignment with what they've been prepared to do on the earth for this great and coming harvest of more than a billion souls.

Our role in heaven is to connect with people on the earth. We're appearing to people more and interacting with some of the people who visit heaven and speaking with them. Whether they come in their minds' eyes or in the Spirit or have a near-death experience, we are interacting with them and giving them messages to take back to the earth. Yes, that's basically what we're doing. Matthew has said before that we will be mentoring many people on the earth. So that is my answer to that question. I hope that's okay.

Nicola: That's awesome, Mary. Thank you so much.

I've had a wonderful interview with you, and I don't know how many pages the book will be. I know Matthew has thirteen more questions, and this interview has taken less than an hour.

9 *What are your final words?*

Well, Nicola, I just want to say again how privileged I am to speak through you. You have trained yourself in the Lord so that you can hear from me, and it's such an honor to hear my voice through a different heart and soul, to have that unique perspective coming through someone else. Matthew's voice and your voice are both unique, and any person we speak through has a unique perspective and way of thinking and speaking that influences what we say. We speak through them, and each of our voices comes through their understanding and their perspective as well as what we are saying. Sometimes what we say will surprise the person whom we are speaking through, and so the person will know that he or she is definitely hearing from us.

I want to say I'm really excited for what's happening on earth. I would like people to prepare and respond to what the Lord is asking them to do right now. I hope they use what God has put in their hand—their talent and their gift—and serve the Lord. I wish people would awaken to the great purposes for their lives and to the great things that will soon happen on this earth. I wish people would see that the time they are in now is like the midnight hour in the sense that there's not much time to prepare.

The church needs to prepare now; it needs to awaken now and be learning the things of the Spirit. The people need to be aware that they are citizens of heaven and that saints are coming down to mentor them and help give them direction. A time will come—and I know you've heard this before, Nicola—when all believers will need to hear individually from the Holy Spirit for themselves. They won't be able to rely on a prophet all the time. They won't have a prophet on hand. They will need the Holy Spirit to guide them. It could cost them their lives if they haven't taken the time to learn how to hear the voice of the Lord for themselves. It's not hard. All people can hear the voice of God for themselves.

That's really what people need to know. They need to know that time is short, and they need to prepare for the harvest and for what God is asking them to do in the harvest. If they don't know what their roles or gifts are, they need to be putting their hands to something until the Lord leads them into what they're specifically meant to do. I know it's hard for some people. They've been alive for years and still don't know what they're supposed to do. If they keep busy, if they put their hands to the plow at whatever is in front of them, they will soon see if it's suited to them or not. The Lord will guide them and show them if this is what he wants them to do. They will have a sense that this is what they are called to do, and the Lord will bless them in it if it is right for them. It's a matter of trying out different things and being aware of the people around them who are suffering.

Unfortunately in your world today, many people focus on what they can buy. Everything revolves around money, but in the Lord's kingdom, everything is upside down. Instead, everything revolves around people and the love for people that the Father has and his heart for them. He wants his church to love like that. He wants them to focus less on buildings and less on big houses and big cars and other unnecessary material possessions. While church buildings are great, he wants his people to use wisdom and not be excessive. He wants his people to focus on what's important to his kingdom and what will bring eternal reward.

There's nothing more important to God than souls. There's nothing more important to God than relieving the suffering of hurting people on earth. He wants his people to reach out to those who are hungry, who are destitute, who are alone, who are widowed, who are grieving, who are suffering, who are suicidal, who are mentally ill, or who are physically disabled. The Lord wants Christians to reach out

21

NICOLA WHITEHALL | MATTHEW ROBERT PAYNE

to so many people, but sometimes Christians are too busy looking at their phones to look up and see the needs around them. They're too busy being busy and rushing to the next meeting or their next job or their next appointment or activity. Busyness seems so important.

But if they open their eyes, they will see that there are people they could touch, people they could prophesy to, like Matthew does with his prophetic evangelism. This opens so many hearts and plants so many seeds that bring fruit. He won't know how great that fruit will be or the outcome of that seed that he planted until he gets to heaven. Then he will realize the importance of the prophetic step he took to share the seed with people: how it took root, how it grew, and how it was harvested so that they became Christians. Christians could encourage so many people. If Christians could learn to hear the voice of the Holy Spirit and step out and learn how to approach people, how to share the heart of God and share their testimony with them, then that would please the Lord. Christians could do this now: just be aware of the people around them and look for a way to bless them.

If you're not comfortable giving prophetic words at this point, that's okay. You can engage a person in conversation. You can give money to a poor person. You can take someone out for dinner. You can invite someone home for lunch. You can give someone clothes or Christmas presents if they are in need. That's what I have to say to the people of this earth.

Nicola: Thank you so much, Mary. It was such an honor to hear from you today. Thank you for speaking through me. I hope I haven't made up too many of the words, and I hope the words I said came from you. I'm quite sure they did. Thank you so much for taking the time to talk to me for about an hour. I'm so privileged to

22

have you come into my house to share your words with me. I really appreciate that. You're such a blessing, Mary Magdalene. Thank you for being such a blessing to Matthew, to me, and to the world with your words.

In Jesus's name, Amen.

Matthew's Questions

1 *How are you feeling today?*

It's an exciting time to come down and speak to you, Matthew. I have been coming down nearly every day to help you with your journals and your homework for your healing. It's good to speak to you daily or once every couple of days and give you messages and spend time with you in heaven together.

I am overjoyed that I have the opportunity to come and speak to the people of the world again. It's a great responsibility to speak to your readers. I look forward to this exciting time.

You had Nicola pick some questions for you, and you picked some questions for yourself. You spoke to your friend Wendy, and she came up with some questions too. Between the three of you, you've come up with some great questions. Nicola has already asked her questions, and she has done a wonderful job so far with the answers that I provided for her. We worked very well together. I was touched that you offered Nicola the opportunity to do a book together. I'm always excited to speak. It's a great privilege to come and speak to the people of the earth, especially the readers of your books.

I find it a real honor to come from heaven to give people an understanding of what I know, what I know about heaven and what I experienced while I was on earth. I love to give people a more complete and thorough look at my life, both now in heaven and when I was on earth.

I lived a really different life, and many people are attracted to my message and to my life. I've had a lot of people wonder about me. Many people have written historical books about me.

They made many assumptions about my life, so I really appreciate the Holy Spirit and God as they allowed me to come to the world and speak and share what's on my mind. They have allowed me to share the truth of what happened in my life and what's happening in heaven.

I look forward to answering the upcoming questions. God bless

2 What is God like?

Scripture says that Jesus was the exact representation of God the Father. (See Hebrews 1:3.) To answer the question really simply: if you know Jesus, you know God.

Jesus came to earth to be a visible and tangible expression of God the Father. Everything that Jesus did, everything that Jesus said, came directly from the Father. In John 5:19, Jesus said that he only did what he saw his Father doing. Jesus said in John 12:49 that the words he spoke were the words of his Father.

Many of you who are listening to this have no idea what God is like. Many of you who are listening to this have a better idea through the Gospels and through preaching of who Jesus was. You understand that Jesus was full of love and compassion and that he loved the broken-hearted and the destitute and hurting. That's what God is like.

Can you imagine being a father and losing touch with your children? You can imagine being an earthly father and going through a marriage breakup like Matthew did. He went through a divorce when his child was eight, and he never saw his child again.

God feels this way about his creation. Many people on earth are God's children, both Christians and non-Christians alike. They are God's children. God is like a father without custody, a father without parental access to his children.

Many people growing up on earth have been abused or have had a bad relationship with their father. They tend to form their concepts about God based on the experiences that they've had with their own earthly father.

Nothing can compare with God. Some people think he is judgmental, angry, and ferocious. They think that he acts harshly. Some aspects of him do demand justice and holiness. But he is like a loving Santa Claus. Children like Santa Claus, and he has a loving grandfatherly manner about him where you want to sit on his lap and get a hug.

God's very much like Santa Claus in that he is so full of love. He just wants his children to come to him with a childlike innocence. So many of us don't approach God with the right understanding. Many of us tend to think that we have all these sins in our lives, and God won't welcome us.

Yet what father would not welcome his son? Even if his son were a murderer or a child abuser, a father would still love his son. A father on earth would still honor and respect his son, no matter what.

We have a Father who loved us so much that he sent his Son to die on the cross to pay the penalty for our sins. If you can't approach God the Father by yourself, you can get to know God the Father through Matthew's books: *Conversations with God: Book 1, Conversations with God Book 2,* and *Conversations with God: Book 3.*

You can read those books and come to experience some of the nature of God that Matthew has come to understand. God is so fun. He has no qualms about ruling heaven. He is full of authority, and yet he is so full of love.

He is like the grandfather at a family gathering that all the children come up to and hug. The grandfather has a whole lot of presents for the children, and they all come up and sit on his lap and unwrap their presents.

If you're close to Jesus, just imagine an older Jesus. Imagine that God is so much like Jesus. Matthew approached God once and started talking to him. It was a relatively new experience for him, but God said that Matthew had been speaking to him all his life. Matthew was surprised. God was saying that as long as Matthew has been talking to Jesus, he has been talking to him. That's who God is. He is not only God the Father, but he is Jesus. So you can approach him through Jesus. If you have a good understanding of who Jesus is, then you'll have a good understanding of who God the Father is.

God gets the bad rap and a bad reputation. He is blamed for so many things: disease, calamities, earthquakes, hurricanes, tsunamis, floods, accidents, car accidents, and cancer. He is blamed for everything.

God is not the cause of these things. In my experience, he is a really loving Father to me. When you come to heaven, it might take a while for you to grow in your healing to a point where you can approach God the Father and sit on his lap and have a beautiful conversation with him.

I appreciate that many of you have father wounds, and yet God the Father is not like any of your fathers.

3 What is it like to have authority in heaven?

The book, *Princess Diana Speaks from Heaven: A Divine Revelation*, speaks about my role in heaven and how I am in a position of authority.

I operate in a similar position to the role of the royal family. It's interesting that Prince Harry got married today just as Matthew is recording this. I operate in a similar manner to a member of the royal family in heaven. I go to official functions and open official events and attend different ceremonies.

Jesus clearly said that he who wants to be great in the kingdom of heaven must be a servant. (See Matthew 20:26.) Much of ruling in heaven is about servanthood. Much of the background of the authority that I possess in heaven comes from working with all the different people of heaven and being a great servant.

We know that Jesus was promoted to have the greatest name above all names and became the King of Kings. He has great authority in heaven. Many of you on earth create prayers and end your prayer in Jesus's name. In other words, you are asking Jesus to make sure that what you pray happens.

Jesus, who has supreme authority in heaven, is still serving humanity and people. Jesus still gets the glory for miracles, signs, and wonders on earth. Jesus is still operating through the power of the Holy Spirit on earth.

Jesus, who has the greatest authority of all, is still the greatest servant in the universe. The point I'm making is that being in a position of authority in heaven isn't something to brag or boast about. This position comes with a lot of responsibility and a lot of laid-down love.

I love the people of heaven and on earth. So many people who have suffered on earth developed their capacity to have great compassion. Jesus carried with him a sense of great compassion that allowed him to do amazing miracles.

I have this compassion and this love that compels me to serve. When I was promoted to heaven at my death, I was given a position of authority as a reward for some of the works I'd done on earth.

I am really pleased to have that authority and to lead and encourage people. I spend time with all sorts of people in heaven. I encourage, bless, and teach people. Nicola said in her interview that I'm a dancer, and I dance and choreograph dances.

I perform ballet and modern dance. I do all kinds of activities. Heaven is not boring. In heaven, you can really stretch your wings and let your hair down, as it were. You truly have the ability to become everything that you are destined to become.

I am the Bride of Christ. I am pleased to have a wonderful friend in Jesus. We've continued a very close relationship in heaven. As I am in close relationship with Jesus in heaven, I tend to share some of his responsibilities there. It's a great honor to serve with him and a great privilege to do some of the work that he has given me to do.

4 *What do you wish people on earth understood about heaven?*

The first thing I want to tell you about heaven is you don't spend all your days in the throne room singing worship to God. You don't spend your time floating on clouds playing harps. You don't spend all your time doing things without any significance.

In heaven, you live the life that you are born to live. Now someone who is a doctor on earth doesn't necessarily have the same position in heaven because there is no sickness in heaven. But some people arrive in heaven with deep emotional wounds, and they carry that pain and hurt into heaven.

Certain people will work with the fresh arrivals to heaven and help them heal and adjust to heaven. Some people who were former doctors on earth might help people heal emotionally. Some people who were counselors on earth will continue to help with the counseling and the transition of people from earth to heaven.

Can you imagine people dying in Africa of disease, of starvation? Some of them have died in tremendous trauma. They have to adjust from being poverty-stricken and in hunger and disease into a perfect heaven, a heaven that operates with enough food for everyone and a great environment with no hardship.

Some people take time to adjust and fit into heaven and get used it. Jesus rules in heaven. The whole of heaven spins on an axis, and the axis is Jesus. If you had no interest in Jesus on earth and if you lived a really carnal life full of degrading sin and evil, you wouldn't like heaven.

Heaven is so full of glory and peace, and your spirit and your soul would resist that. It would be like torture for you. In some respects, it's more plausible that truly evil people go to the outer darkness or hell.

All the people in heaven have jobs. If you've read a number of Matthew's books, you'd know that they have jobs to do and perform.

Princess Diana shared about fashion in heaven, and everyone has the ability to choose their own clothing. You have wardrobes in heaven full of lovely clothes. The food is glorious. You can eat to your heart's content.

Some people talk about going on a cruise and how on a cruise line, food is available all the time. That's their idea of paradise. If you like food, heaven will really bless you. There are many restaurants and all types of foods that can be created. You can have a function in your house and have it catered with a catering team.

You can cook in your own house. When you're finished with your meals, the plates, dishes, pots, and pans are washed up and put away through a miracle. You don't have to do dishes or collect trash in heaven. No one in heaven has to clean toilets.

Most of the cleaning is done supernaturally. You won't have to do the laborious jobs in heaven that you do on earth, jobs like ironing, washing dishes, cooking, and other menial jobs.

Many people on earth actually do start to do what they were born to do on earth. When they get to heaven, many of them will continue to live out their life's purpose. Matthew is a teacher. He will teach and instruct people in heaven.

He is a writer, and he'll write books in heaven. There are great libraries in heaven. You can have a library in your house of all the books you've ever read and all the books you're interested in reading. All the accepted books available on Amazon are all available in heaven except for erotic fiction or horror.

You can learn from people who went before you on earth or people who have discovered more than you in the Christian faith on earth. You can be in heaven and learn from them. In heaven, you can hear a lecture by Paul the apostle, the disciples, and the prophets of the Old Testament. You can learn from them.

You can learn from gifted teachers in heaven. Many people don't even know their names as they are not well-known. You can do and enjoy so many things in heaven. Of course, you will have the opportunity to go to the throne room and spend time in the presence of God.

The presence of God in the throne room is amazing, and many times, you'll find yourself on your face, worshipping God. Everything you can think of is catered to in heaven. Everyone in heaven is learning more and more—each week, every week—in earth time. There's no time in heaven, but every week in earth time in heaven, you are closer and closer to the Lord. You fall deeper and deeper in love with the Lord, and you become more and more experienced as a heavenly being as you spend more time in heaven.

5 What relationship do you have with children in heaven?

Princess Diana has a wonderful relationship with children in heaven. Jesus has an amazing relationship with children in heaven. I have worked with children, mixed with children, and spent time with them, but I wouldn't say that that they are my primary responsibility.

The children of heaven are innocent and pure. They are like little angels, especially those who have been aborted, who never had a life on earth. They weren't born with a sin nature. They have never sinned and have grown up in the atmosphere of heaven.

They really shine, and they have amazing personalities and tremendous love. They are so much more advanced than children on earth. In heaven, they have been shown the crucifixion and the life of Christ. The actual life of Jesus can be played to them like a hologram. They can sit with a group of children and the disciples, and Jesus can talk to them and teach them. This can all appear like a hologram to the children. They are actually taken back in time to witness Jesus, and they see it as a hologram.

The children can be right there and experience it. The children of heaven are just a joy to see and a delight to spend time with. I have a lot of official functions that keep me busy. So I don't have much to say about this question.

6 *How did your life change after meeting Jesus on earth?*

Many people are not aware that I was a high-class prostitute when I was on earth. My life was radically different before I met Jesus and changed drastically after I met him.

Jesus knew and understood what I did. I went to confess my sins to him, poured oil on his feet, and washed his feet with my tears. As recorded in Luke 7:37, I was the woman with the alabaster container of expensive oil.

I just lived to hear Jesus and to be in his presence from that time on. I was enraptured by Jesus as I had a lot of money and had traveled the world to listen to the world's best speakers and best philosophers.

I understood what good teaching was. I understood knowledge and wisdom. I was just blown away by Jesus, but more than even his knowledge, I was blown away by the person that he was.

There wasn't one person that Jesus didn't love. He had very vocal enemies. They were rude, mean, and vicious, yet he responded to them with love. Jesus heard what people said and was able to process forgiveness on the spot.

It wasn't that he didn't hear what they said. He was just so loving, and he proved that he was perfect by the way he loved his enemies. It was such a privilege to be with Jesus and to see him demonstrate the love of God when it came to people.

He changed me. I changed my experiences with men: intimacy with men, men using my body, and men saying that they were in love with me. I changed in my relationships to a brotherly love with no sex. I'd experienced the different sort of love than the love that Jesus expressed. Jesus had this totally unconditional, unselfish, unrelenting love for people.

He just loved people and was so amazing. It didn't take many weeks of being around him for me to fall for him and love him. I truly fell in love with Jesus. When I found out that Jesus was not going to marry anyone, I tempered down my love.

I know that Matthew really loves Jesus, but as a woman, you might love Jesus romantically. He was good-looking to me although Isaiah 53 says that he wasn't good to look at.

I'd had all sorts of men grope my body and use me. They ranged from the really handsome to the grotesque. Looks weren't important to me, but Jesus's heart shone. He had a glow on his skin. They say he shone like the sun when he came off the Mount of Transfiguration. (See Matthew 17:1–12.) To me, Jesus always had a shine and a sheen on his skin. He was just so full of love. He totally transformed my life. I decided that I didn't want any men unless I could have Jesus.

I'd met so many men in my profession, and I'd seen the depravity of men, their baseness and cruelty. I was pretty broken by the relationships I'd had with men before Jesus. Jesus just looked into my eyes and held my face. He healed those wounds.

I shed many tears. One look from Jesus just touched you in such a deep place. Can you imagine meeting Jesus face to face? Can you imagine him holding your chin in his hands and him just looking at you with overwhelming love coming from his eyes? Can you imagine how you'd feel?

Well, I had that situation played out many, many times, and he totally revolutionized my life. I set one of my goals to become like him, to live like he did, to walk like he did, and to love others like he did.

Some good men were among his disciples, as I mentioned through Nicola. John was especially nice, and I loved him. But there was something about Jesus. There was something that resonated so deeply with me about him. He was just liquid love in a body.

He had his challenging and hard times, times when he felt sad. I was able to cheer him up and joke with him, as I shared with Nicola.

I was glad that he was vulnerable with me. We grew closer and closer together. He had a remarkable influence on me just as I had an influence on him. I'd been with many men. I knew how to set a man's mind at ease.

I could be there for him from time to time in some measure, but he totally and radically impacted my life. I was so pleased I was on earth when he came to visit the first time.

7 What was it like to lose Jesus, to witness his death?

I shared with Nicola that it was difficult to see him whipped and to witness his death. The word difficult doesn't begin to capture it. Imagine if someone came with a big fork that you use to spear meat, and I grabbed that fork and plunged it in to your heart and ripped out your heart. That's the feeling that I felt when I watched Jesus dying on the cross. It was as though someone had ripped out my heart.

I knew that he was going to die. I knew that he was going to be crucified. He told me beforehand that he would be crucified. I'd understood that. Matthew and I covered that in Book 1, *Mary Magdalene Speaks from Heaven: A Divine Revelation*.

But as he died, I felt as if my heart were being ripped out as I watched the agony that he was in. I had this really close relationship with Jesus. I was as close as a male and a female could be, even closer than married males and females. We were like soulmates with a very intimate connection.

I was losing half of myself, a part of myself. Mary, his mother, was grief-stricken at the crucifixion. I spent some of my time consoling his mother and other people, which was just a natural reaction because my heart was so wrecked. My heart was broken, wrenched out of me.

I was really hard to console. I went into the beginning of a deep depression because the lover of my soul had been taken. I know that Jesus promised me that he'd visit me; he'd visit me in visions, in appearances, and in encounters.

He had promised me that I'd see him again. I was a bit surprised to see him on resurrection day and to be a witness to him rising again. I was honored to be able to share with the disciples that he had risen from the grave, and he was alive again.

They had a problem with believing me at first and had to laugh that a woman brought them the news. But I must have said something convincing because they rushed off to the grave to see if my story was true, and they found the stone rolled away.

It was heart-wrenching to lose Jesus. It helped me cling to the Holy Spirit and use the Holy Spirit to commune with Jesus and the Father. I grew at a supernatural and accelerated pace because when Jesus was gone, I wanted to talk to him all the time in heaven. I wanted to walk with him, talk with him, and share my heart with him.

It was like a divorce. One person in a divorce always seems to be left behind. One partner normally leaves the other partner, and the other partner is heartbroken and can't come to grips with the loss.

The same thing happened with me and Jesus. I was just brokenhearted and almost beyond consolation. John, Peter, and some of the disciples tried to console me. But the baptism, the infilling, and communication with the Holy Spirit allowed me to get my life back together. I was able to move forward to find an even keel again.

I became very mystical and used to have many encounters with the risen Jesus and see him in visions. We'd walk and talk together. I used to spend a lot of time visiting heaven. I became what modern people would call a mystic, someone who was enraptured with God and everything of God.

I became living love. I become known for having the love of Jesus. I came to express the love of Jesus in a really beautiful and caring way.

This was the example that Jesus played in my life. He came to earth and spent time demonstrating what love was. I took full advantage of his lessons and was his very best student. I listened intently to what he said. I questioned him about his motives and the reasons behind what he said. I was one of his hungriest followers. When he left, I put all of the lessons that I learned into practice.

8 Can you take us back to the early church just after Jesus died?

When Jesus died, the disciples were crushed. Up until the third day when he rose again, then Jesus started appearing to the disciples and spent forty days with them until he ascended, and the disciples were jubilant. Then came another sad time because Jesus had ascended and left them, and they felt like orphans. They felt like I did when Jesus died.

Then Pentecost came, and they were baptized in the Holy Spirit. The Holy Spirit came powerfully among them. They started to preach in boldness. They started to share about Jesus and his resurrection and boldly proclaimed the gospel.

This was especially meaningful to the poor, the brokenhearted, and the commoners. The gospel seemed to spread more quickly and be more easily understood by the poor than it was by the rich. I guess it's still the same in America now: people with wealth and money seem to think that money can answer all their questions. They're not as responsive to the gospel as the poor are.

The gospel seemed to spread. I had a lot of clients that I used to see. In today's money, some people spent $250,000 for a weekend with me. I began to share the gospel with them.

I used to tell them that I left my profession for a man that I came to love, Jesus Christ. I told them about him and shared his teachings. I told them that he was crucified and that he had risen again.

I prophesied and shared a message from Jesus with them. They were deeply touched. Many of the men that used me as clients became Christians through my witness. I ate dinner with them and shared the gospel plainly and simply with them. I was truthful and shared my love. I was the Mary that they loved, and yet I wasn't charging them for my time.

The men understood that there was an exchange, a trading of time. An exchange happened. Some of the men responded to my words. About half of my former clients became Christians. Many of them were wealthy and gave to the early church. The early church seemed to be funded by many of these men. They had tremendous land holdings and wealth.

This brought a lot of funds to the early church. The early church was financed to look after the homeless, the poor, the needy, the sick, and the hurting. Of course, the gifts of healing were flowing through Peter and the disciples.

Peter had a healing gift. He could walk around Jerusalem, and his shadow would fall on people on the sidewalk, healing them. He could heal thousands of people every day. He had a real reputation for that. People used to come from other countries to be healed by Peter.

The disciples picked up the ability to heal. In church history, Peter wasn't the only one whose shadow could heal people.

As the apostles and the Christians grew, it was a real hot bed of learning and instruction. New Christians came into the fellowship and were interested in the gifts of the Spirit. Many people who'd been healed were impressed with the fact that they were healed, and they wanted the ability to heal too.

They often received the gift of healing through faith and started to heal people. It was like a match had been lit in a dry forest. The gospel just spread like fire. It was exciting. The wealth of my clients supplied us with money, which was like supplying oxygen to a fire. The money, the miracles, and the love that was expressed by the early church for one another were simply remarkable to see.

I continued evangelizing my former clients. I had a little bit of a reputation for being a mystic and a Jesus follower. I learned to spend quality time with Jesus and the Father. I learned to spend time by myself with them to be refreshed in the tradition of Jesus spending time with the Father. Every morning, I spent time with God and Jesus in devotions.

I could heal, prophesy, and move in the gifts of the Holy Spirit. The church just blossomed. It took off and exploded.

Real love was shared between the brethren. There were no fights over doctrine, and no disputes over what different verses meant. We talked about Jesus and had him in common. In the early days, it was exciting.

We were like a family of love going forth. As the family grew, people started to give of their property like it says in Acts 4:32–35.

We kept their properties and then sold them. The money went into the kingdom, and more people were fed and taken care of.

Acts 2:47 says that people were added to the number every single day. It was an exciting time for the gospel, an exciting time to be alive. I was really pleased to be in the middle of it.

9 *What would you like to share with anyone that identifies with you?*

Don't waste any time getting to know Jesus. Start with the Gospels of Matthew, Mark, Luke, and John and try and understand Jesus. Spending time in the Gospels is definitely a great way to get to know Jesus.

But rather than just reading them over one day, try and meditate on them and read them for a year. Ask yourself some questions: "What did Jesus mean by this? How did Jesus feel when he did this? How did Jesus feel when he said this? What was the point of him saying this?" Do a deep study into the life of Jesus.

Matthew's written a book called, *The Parables of Jesus Made Simple: Updated and Expanded Edition*, that will help you understand what Jesus was teaching. He's also written, *Jesus Speaking Today*, which will give you insight into who Jesus is. He has another book called *Finding Intimacy with Jesus Made Simple*, which will encourage you and tell you more about Jesus.

Jesus is really worth getting to know. It's hard to describe Jesus in words. Princess Diana did a nice job of describing Jesus in

Princess Diana Speaks from Heaven. Diana shares what Jesus is like in heaven.

Jesus really does make the best friend that you can have and will easily listen to you. He has all the time in the world to listen to you. If you can learn to speak to Jesus, Matthew had a book on how to hear God speak. If you can learn to speak to Jesus and speak to God, it'd be tremendous.

Jesus is the answer to your life. I want to share with you that he's not a waste of time. He is still the focal point of my life. I love him and honor him so much in heaven. He uses me effectively there.

Of course, you want to get to know the Father and develop a relationship with him. Once again, I'd encourage you to have a two-way speaking relationship with the Father. You can gain some insight in to the Father through *Conversations with God: Book 1, Conversations with God: Book 2,* and *Conversations with God: Book 3.* In those books, Matthew had conversations with the Father about certain subjects. You get to see some of the Father's heart.

It'd be really encouraging if you come to know the Father and develop a two-way conversational relationship with him. Of course, you can come to know the Holy Spirit and learn his voice. I want to share this important information with you.

So many people think that they know Jesus, but they don't really know him. The same could be said about millions of people who think they know Donald Trump. They might have read books by Donald Trump. They could've seen every press release about Donald Trump. They could have heard every speech that Donald Trump has given, but they don't know him.

They don't know what sort of toilet paper he likes. They don't know what his favorite foods are. They don't know how he likes to relax. They don't know how he treats people when he's one-on-one with them. They don't know that he asks many questions when he's in an audience of people. They don't know so many things about him.

Similarly, so many Christians don't know about Jesus. I encourage you to get to know Jesus. Do whatever you can to get to know him because he really is the answer to your life. He captivated me, and nothing is stopping him from captivating you also. I would really love to see you press into Jesus and to get to know him on a deep and intimate level.

I knew Jesus, grew really close to him, and become one of his best friends. But you can also. It's possible to become a close friend of Jesus. You can become so close to Jesus that he would come and visit you, talk to you, minister to you, and walk beside you as you walk down the street. He would hold your hand, tell you wonderful things, and give you great blessings in the conversations that he has with you.

I really think that Jesus is the center of the universe. I encourage you to read his Gospels. Take the resources that I've offered and find out about Jesus, find out about the Father. Develop an ability to talk back and forth with each member of the Trinity one by one. Get to know them. Do what they tell you to do.

Matthew has a book that I recommend to you called *7 Keys to Intimacy with Jesus*. Read it. Put the teachings into practice and develop a life that is very close and intimate with Jesus, and you will do very well.

10 *What is your message to the outcast, to people the church doesn't accept?*

If you're one of those people—a gambler, a heavy drinker, addicted to pornography, an adulterer, a homosexual, or in the sex industry—Jesus can heal you. You might need to make a public confession and turn away from your sin before the church would accept you. But this is my message to you. Jesus can touch your heart and minister to you. Depending on the trauma in your life, you might need special counseling and someone to work with you on your healing.

Making Jesus your best friend is a great idea. How do you become best friends with Jesus? Well, how do you do that with regular people? You spend time with them and talk to them back and forth.

I encourage you to learn about Jesus's life, to read the resources we quoted about Jesus's life, and to develop the ability to talk to Jesus. I know that he would talk to you and gently guide you through your life and encourage you because Jesus is the answer. He has the answer for many things.

"I am the way, the truth, and the life," said Jesus in John 14:6. He has the way; he is the truth, and he can provide you with the meaning of life. Jesus is the answer.

So many people from different backgrounds, different sin lifestyles, have a reason for why they are doing what they do. Someone committing adultery might love the new person more than the current wife or the current husband. There might be problems in their marriage that caused them to look elsewhere.

As I shared with Nicola, women are in the sex trade for many reasons, not all of them good ones. My heart goes out to these women in the sex trade. Jesus really is the answer. He is my answer.

He healed my heart. I was a prostitute. I had a broken heart. Jesus mended my heart, healed me, and transformed me from broken to full of love, with great friends, and solid, long-lasting relationships. You can change from being broken-hearted to full of love and compassion with tremendous friends and become a lasting influence.

That's who God wants you to be: full of love, influential, and able to make an impact on the world. He doesn't want you to drown in your own blood with a sucking heart wound, but he wants you to be alive and vibrant with a healthy heart. He doesn't want your heart to be troubled, but he wants you to blow bubbles of joy.

You can change. You can be transformed. Jesus can hold your hand. You can be gay, and Jesus can be your friend for years and years and years before you decide to change your lifestyle.

Jesus will be your friend and will love you even in the midst of what the church and Christians would call sin. Jesus can love you exactly where you're at. He can mend and heal your heart and lead you to people who can counsel you so that you can become whole.

Jesus has answers. He's helping Matthew at the moment. He led Matthew to a helpful counselor. Jesus cares. He's holding Matthew's hand as Matthew receives healing and goes through trauma in his past.

He really does have answers. He cares and has the solution for your life.

I want to encourage you to seek him out and to learn to speak back and forth with him. I want to encourage you to take a risk on Jesus and allow him to be your friend and to speak to you. Allow him to guide and direct you. I hope that helped.

11 *What are you most interested in about the times and seasons coming to earth?*

A time is coming to earth when Isaiah 60:1–7 will be fulfilled.

"Arise, shine; For your light has come!

And the glory of the Lord is risen upon you.

For behold, the darkness shall cover the earth,

And deep darkness the people;

But the Lord will arise over you,

And His glory will be seen upon you.

The Gentiles shall come to your light,

And kings to the brightness of your rising.

'Lift up your eyes all around, and see:

They all gather together, they come to you;

Your sons shall come from afar,

And your daughters shall be nursed at your side.

Then you shall see and become radiant,

And your heart shall swell with joy;

Because the abundance of the sea shall be turned to you,

The wealth of the Gentiles shall come to you.

The multitude of camels shall cover your land,

The dromedaries of Midian and Ephah;

All those from Sheba shall come;

They shall bring gold and incense,

And they shall proclaim the praises of the Lord.

All the flocks of Kedar shall be gathered together to you,

The rams of Nebaioth shall minister to you;

They shall ascend with acceptance on My altar,

And I will glorify the house of My glory.'"

A time will come, as this verse says, when "the glory of the Lord is going to come upon people." That means that people will be walking down the street with their faces shining like the sun. Everyone who sees them will know that God is with them.

This is going to come upon earth in the future. It's been prophesied. I've seen Matthew's face shine like the sun. He's experienced it a number of times. A season will come on earth when the sons of God will arise. They will take dominion, and they will prosper in the world. I look forward to this time and season in the world.

I look forward to times on earth when the people of God will really shine and stand out to the people of the world. The world, according to Isaiah 60, will have to become pretty dark, and that's when the people will shine. You can see now how the world is growing darker.

The world is totally ignoring God's commandments. People refuse to submit to the ways of God. Society is becoming more and more off-track.

As the world plunges into darkness, the Christian church will start to arise as the Christian church is persecuted a little bit and comes under more pressure. Christians will become bolder and bolder. They will start to develop the gifts of the Holy Spirit. They will start to walk in power. They will begin to increase in inventing new things.

Many Christians will receive business ideas and start businesses. Many ministries will start up and be funded by people in business. People in business will launch out into ministry and succeed in both business and ministry.

A whole number of fire-breathing Christians will be in the world. So many Christians will be able to speak the truth, boldly proclaim the truth. So many Christians will start businesses, start inventions, and be successful.

Christians will create businesses as big as Apple, as big as Facebook, just as the darkness closes in. Certain Christians, certain movements of Christians, will have influence. Certain Christians will take the world by force and by storm.

A real battle is going on, a real battle in the cosmos in the second heaven where Satan dwells. This will be a battle between the forces of good and evil.

Satan will try and close down the world to work with his dark angels and principalities to direct mankind and make the world become darker. At the same time, light will erupt, and more and more Christians will arise. More and more Christians will become successful and powerful. More millionaires and billionaires will be in the Christian church. An exciting war will be going on. Evangelists will come out of nowhere with miracles, signs, and wonders. There will be revival in the world.

Ministries and revivals will happen from stadium to stadium, city to city. It's been prophesied. Heaven agrees that a nameless, faceless generation will rise up. Powerful prophets and preachers will rise up with no name and no reputation, and they will take cities by storm.

A holy war will start because the enemy knows that time is closing in and coming to an end. Exciting times are coming.

]It's been a real honor to be here today, Matthew. It's been so exciting to talk to you and address some of the details that we've covered. I guess you could sum up what I've said in these interviews in one sentence: the answer is Jesus. The whole of heaven rotates on the axis of Jesus.

Jesus is really the way, the truth, and the life. You find eternal life when you enter through Jesus. Jesus is the answer to the universe, the answer to man's problems.

You want to head to the destination of God, his Father. God is a beautiful Father. I encourage people to get to know him as Father.

I love you. I love the people who've been reading this book or listening to it. I encourage you to check out all the resources in the links and Matthew's books that I've suggested. I encourage you to go further and read those books and do your research. I encourage you to seek out Jesus, learn from him, and be encouraged by his life. Do yourself a favor and learn and take the time to learn how to speak to him back and forth so that you can have a walking, talking relationship with Jesus.

Learn to experience visions. Both Praying Medic and Michael Van Vlymen have books on how to see in the spirit. Get those books. Learn how to see in the spirit so that you can have visions, entertain Jesus, see Jesus, and interact with him.

I encourage you to spend your time and your life seeking Jesus and going after him because Jesus really is my Lord. He's my savior. He's my king. He's my redeemer. He's my soul mate. He's my husband. He's everything to me. I encourage you to develop a relationship where he's everything to you too.

12 *What are your final words?*

It's been a real honor to be here today, Matthew. It's been so exciting to talk to you and address some of the details that we've covered. I guess you could sum up what I've said in these interviews in one sentence: the answer is Jesus. The whole of heaven rotates on the axis of Jesus.

Jesus is really the way, the truth, and the life. You find eternal life when you enter through Jesus. Jesus is the answer to the universe, the answer to man's problems.

You want to head to the destination of God, his Father. God is a beautiful Father. I encourage people to get to know him as Father.

I love you. I love the people who've been reading this book or listening to it. I encourage you to check out all the resources in the links and Matthew's books that I've suggested. I encourage you to go further and read those books and do your research. I encourage you to seek out Jesus, learn from him, and be encouraged by his life. Do yourself a favor and learn and take the time to learn how to speak to him back and forth so that you can have a walking, talking relationship with Jesus.

Learn to experience visions. Both Praying Medic and Michael Van Vlymen have books on how to see in the spirit. Get those books. Learn how to see in the spirit so that you can have visions, entertain Jesus, see Jesus, and interact with him.

I encourage you to spend your time and your life seeking Jesus and going after him because Jesus really is my Lord. He's my savior. He's my king. He's my redeemer. He's my soul mate. He's my husband. He's everything to me. I encourage you to develop a relationship where he's everything to you too.

I'd love to hear from you…

One of the ways that you can bless me as a writer is by writing an honest and candid review of my book on Amazon. I always read the reviews of my books, and I would love to hear what you have to say about this one.

Before I buy a book, I read the reviews first. You can make an informed decision about a book when you have read enough honest reviews from readers. One way to help me sell this book and to give me positive feedback is by writing a review for me. It doesn't cost you a thing but helps me and the future readers of this book enormously.

To read my blog, request a life-coaching session, request your own personal prophecy, or to receive a personal message from your angel, or to receive your own personal destiny scroll, you can also visit my website at *http://personal-prophecy-today.com* All of the funds raised through my ministry website will go toward the books that I write and self-publish.

To write to me about this book or to share any other thoughts, please feel free to contact me at my personal email address at *survivors.sanctuary@gmail.com.*

You can also friend request me on Facebook at Matthew Robert Payne. Please send me a message if we have no friends in common as a lot of scammers now send me friend requests.

You can also do me a huge favor and share this book on Facebook as a recommended book to read. This will help me and other readers.

How to Sponsor a Book Project

If you have been blessed by this book, you might consider sponsoring a book for me. It normally costs me between fifteen hundred and two thousand dollars or more to produce each book that I write, depending on the length of the book.

If you seek the Holy Spirit about financing a book for me, I know that the Lord would be eternally grateful to you. Consider how much this book has blessed you and then think of hundreds or even thousands of people who would be blessed by a book of mine. As you are probably aware, the vast majority of my books are ninety-nine cents on Kindle, which proves to you that book writing is indeed a ministry for me and not a money-making venture. I would be very happy if you supported me in this.

If you have any questions for me or if you want to know what projects I am currently working on that your money might finance, you can write to me at *survivors.sanctuary@gmail.com* and ask me for more information. I would be pleased to give you more details about my projects.

You can sow any amount to my ministry by simply sending me money via the PayPal link at this address: *http://personal-prophecy-today.com/support-my-ministry/*

You can be sure that your support, no matter the amount, will be used for the publishing of helpful Christian books for people to read.

Acknowledgments by Nicola

God, Jesus, and the Holy Spirit

I want to thank you for guiding and protecting me throughout my life and saying such encouraging things to help me when I struggle or despair in life. Thank you for saving my life when I was seventeen and for allowing me to hold on to you through the hard times. Thank you for your consistent, unchanging love even when I was hateful and unlovely. You are my rock.

My Parents

Thank you for encouraging me in my gifts and talents when I was young and for passing on your gifts and love of writing to me. I have learned so much from both your writing gifts. Thank you for caring for me and persevering with me throughout some of the more difficult stages of my life. I love you both.

Cheryl Devadhar

I want to thank you so much, Cheryl, for being so open and accepting when I first shared with you about meeting saints. You have been my friend for eighteen years and have always stuck by me through thick and thin even when I was in the hospital and lashed out at those who loved me. You are kind, gracious, loyal, and always loving and are willing to keep an open mind regarding new concepts and ways of thinking. Thanks for your amazing support and for listening to me talk about my first coauthored book.

Matthew Robert Payne

Thank you for sharing your wonderful gift of friendship with me. Thank you for opening up your heart and for giving me the chance to be a part of the prophetic team on your website. Thank you for letting me proofread your books and now coauthor with you. I really look up to you.

Lisa Thompson

Thank you for editing this book to your professional standards. Thank you for working with me as a proofreader and for being so gracious with me as I learn. Thank you for teaching me so much. I love your bright, passionate, and loving personality

Acknowledgments by Matthew

I wish to thank the Trinity for their help in my life and with this book. I want to thank my ministry supporters who have helped me publish this book. Without you, nothing could be achieved by me. I want to thank Mary Gibson for the cover. I want to thank my friends: Lisa, Wendy, Mary, Nicola, David, and Michael. And last of all, I want to thank my parents, Bob and June Payne, for loving and supporting me.

Other Books by Matthew Robert Payne

- The Prophetic Supernatural Experience
- Prophetic Evangelism Made Simple
- Your Identity in Christ
- His Redeeming Love: A Memoir
- Writing and Self-Publishing Christian Nonfiction
- Coping with your Pain and Suffering
- Living for Eternity
- Jesus Speaking Today
- Great Cloud of Witnesses Speak
- My Radical Encounters with Angels
- Finding Intimacy with Jesus Made Simple
- My Radical Encounters with Angels: Book Two
- A Beginner's Guide to the Prophetic
- Michael Jackson Speaks from Heaven
- 7 Keys to Intimacy with Jesus
- Conversations with God: Book 1
- Optimistic Visions of Revelation
- Conversations with God: Book 2
- Finding Your Purpose in Christ
- Influencing your World for Christ: Practical Everyday Evangelism
- Deep Calls unto Deep: Answering Questions on the Prophetic
- My Visits to the Galactic Council of Heaven
- The Parables of Jesus Made Simple: Updated and Expanded Edition
- Great Cloud of Witnesses Speak: Old and New

Other Books by Matthew Robert Payne

- Walking under an Open Heaven
- A Message from My Angel: Book 1
- Interviews with the Two Witnesses: Enoch and Elijah Speak
- Gaining Freedom from Sex Addictions: Breaking Free of Pornography and Prostitutes
- Mary Magdalene Speaks from Heaven: A Divine Revelation
- Princess Diana Speaks from Heaven: A Divine Revelation
- How to Hear God's Voice: Keys to Conversational Two-Way Prayer
- Apostle John Speaks from Heaven: A Divine Revelation
- What I Believe
- Great Cloud of Witnesses Speak: God's Generals
- Apostle Peter Speaks from Heaven: A Divine Revelation
- King David Speaks from Heaven: A Divine Revelation
- Twenty-Two Signs that You're Called to Be a Prophet
- Nineteen Scriptures to Change Your Life Forever
- Five Keys to Successful Writing; How I Write One Book per Month
- Apostle Paul Speaks from Heaven: A Divine Revelation

You can find my published books on my Amazon author page.

Upcoming Books

Getting Right with God: Exploring Intimacy through Daily Journaling in the Courts of Heaven

About Matthew Robert Payne

Matthew was raised in a Baptist church and was led to the Lord at the tender age of eight. He has experienced some pain and darkness in his life, which have given him a deep compassion and love for all people.

Today, he's a founding member and admin of a Facebook group called "Prophetic Training Group," and he invites you to join him there. Matthew has a commission from the Lord to train up prophets and to mentor others in the Christian faith. He does this through his Facebook posts and by writing relevant books on the Christian faith.

God originally commissioned him to write at least fifty books in his life, but that has now increased to ninety books. He spends his days writing and earning the money to self-publish. You can support him by donating money at *http://personal-prophecy-today.com* or by requesting any of the other services available through his ministry website.

Recently, the Lord has put it on his heart to start his own publishing company for other people's books to be called Christian Book Publishing USA. It is Matthew's hope to help some people self-publish their books in the future.

It is Matthew's prayer that this book has blessed you, and he hopes it will lead you into a deeper and more intimate relationship with God.

www.ingramcontent.com/pod-product-compliance
Lightning Source LLC
Chambersburg PA
CBHW060145050426
42448CB00010B/2305